WITHOUT REMISSION

Without Remission

Selected Poems by

Walter Helmut Fritz

Translated from the German
by Ewald Osers

LONDON
THE MENARD PRESS
1981

WITHOUT REMISSION

©1981 English translation Ewald Osers

The German poem on page 48 is from Schwierige Überfahrt published by Hoffmann und Campe to whom acknowledgements are gratefully made.

All rights reserved

ISBN 0 903400 66 9

The Menard Press is a member of ALP

Menard Press books are distributed in the United States by
SPD INC: 1636 Ocean View Ave., Kensington, Cal. 94707

COVER: Morandi, *Still Life,* 1946. The Tate Gallery, London.

The Menard Press
8 The Oaks, Woodside Avenue
London N12 8AR

Printed in England by
Skelton's Press Limited
Wellingborough, Northants

For Mechthild

Contents

Introduction   9
Words in the Dark   11
Elsewhere   12
Ancient Representation of Astronomy   13
Soon without Name   14
Cain   15
Late   16
Dam up the Years   17
At the Menhirs in Corsica   18
Janus   19
Ravaged by Pain   20
Mountain Scenery   21
In the Jewish Cemetery in Worms   22
Tomb of the Hunt and Fishing at Tarquinia   23
A Piece of Driftwood   24
What I Know   25
Columbus   26
The Earth on a Photograph   27
Transformations   28
On the Wall of the House   29
But why don't we Scream?   30
Deserted Village   31
Morning in the City   32
Rainy Day on the Beach   33
Morning   34
On Reading Leonardo's Philosophical Diaries   35
Michelangelo   36
Domenico di Bartolo   38
Misfortune   39

Snow   40
Pretexts   41
Shadow of Hope   42
Wind-blown Sand Everywhere   43
A Fool   44
The Child   45
On Returning to our Flat   46
Morandi   47
The Hangman's House   48
Montaigne   49
Die Sonne im Dorf   50
The Sun in the Village   51
Reflection of Flames   52
And So On   53
Difficult Cross   54
Don Juan   55
Gislebertus of Autun: Eve   56
from a cycle: Love Poems   57
Trap   59

Introduction

Just as good wine needs no bush, so good poetry, even in translation, should need no introduction. Especially if it is part of that common Western heritage which English letters, essentially, share with those of continental Europe. I believe that the poetry of a country less than 500 miles away can, and should, be allowed to speak for itself, without the kind of exegesis that might be appropriate to Chinese, Japanese or African poetry.

This belief is, I hope, entirely free from hubris. To claim that translated poetry is fully equivalent to the original would not only be patently foolish but would also suggest a lack of the kind of humility that, I would suggest, must be part of the creative make-up of the literary translator. One can only hope that one has caught and reproduced enough of the original to convey a truthful and accurate picture and to produce in the reader of the translation something approaching the effect that the German poem has on the reader of the original.

A translator of poetry is continually questioned on the reasons for his choice of poet. Why this particular poet and not another? Is this poet 'greater' or 'more important' than that one? I confess that I have always found myself totally unable to answer that question. It has always seemed to me as unanswerable as the question: What made you fall in love with *this* girl? The process that makes a translator of poetry decide that he will – 'must' might not be too strong a word – translate a particular poem or poet is, to my mind, very much like falling in love. A quickening of the pulse, perhaps, on reading the original, a sense of identification, a desire to 'possess' the poem by translating it – in short: instinctive responses rather than 'quality seals' stuck on the poet by reviewers and literary critics.

This is not to belittle the native critics: they are infinitely more knowledgeable about the general literary scene than the translator living in another country could ever hope to be. But the first stimulus must come from inside the translator: only his conviction that he must translate a particular poem holds out any promise of success.

Walter Helmut Fritz today is, of course, a very well known German poet. But I confess to considerable gratification at the thought that I first found myself 'switched on' by his work some years ago, when he had published only two or three volumes of verse, long before he acquired his present fame and honours, and the accolade of having his Collected Poems published at the age of 50.

Fritz is a reticent poet. He is as quiet and undemonstrative in his poetry as he is as an individual. His poetry does not shout, it does not startle, it does not smash idols and it does not call for the overthrow of anything. The conviction it carries stems, I suggest, from an intense inwardness, from a sense of place and time, from a deep awareness of the continuity of civilization, and from a mastery (almost unnoticed because of its inconspicuous perfection) of his language. His notes are soft but their pitch is so sure that they continue to ring long after one has read Fritz's lines.

E.O.

Words in the Dark

Do you notice
how the words
change their shape
in this darkness

growing larger

revealing themselves
more clearly

how they're ahead of us

listening with us for
what's to come

Elsewhere

The island
just visible as an outline
in the distance
between the ropes of the rigging –
a thought
emerging elsewhere
under another name.

Ancient Representation of Astronomy

This loggia with the
view of the stars.
In a niche
the model of the celestial globe,
surrounded by cherubs
with plumbline and footrule,
sextants, optical instruments,
and the assistants
entering the results
in a ledger.
The wish to get to
the far side of nature.
Light whence?
Scarcely more than concealed terror.

Soon without Name

Borderland, not invented,
ageing from Hof to Travemünde.

Mistrust, unyielding, stifling,
between minefield, guard-tower and barbed wire.

Rail-track, in the foot-tangling thicket,
ending and rusting.
Uncontradicted void.

They've burned the forest down
to get a clear field of fire.

Camouflage. Night an accomplice.
The houses turn away
as you pass them.

Land of forgotten roads, of secret smugglers,
land, soon without name.

Cain

He no longer walks
across the fields, a ploughman,
he needs no cudgel.

He no longer asks
in arrogant manner
whether he is
his brother's keeper.

He is no longer
unstable or fugitive.

He wears masks,
in perfect likeness
of his own likeness:
of indifference.

Late

Late the day decided
to linger awhile.

Its counsel
was hard to understand.

The people
spoke very little.

One silence led to another.

How quickly winter comes
among the words.

Dam up the Years

To dam up
the years
which hurtle
down from these
rocky heights
without remission.

At the Menhirs in Corsica

Men worked these stones,
hinted at eye-sockets, nose, ear,
placed them in rows and circles
and tried to divine
how to continue from a beginning.
Wild pear-blossom hangs over them now,
the bees are already at work.

Janus

Pale day,
darkness just over,
darkness soon.

The door,
above it two faces.

This way, that way,
into both distances.

Passages, numberless.

Day, darkness,
a change
in the faces.

The door
for entry
for exit.

Into the beginning
into the end
of the pale day.

Ravaged by Pain

Hate, defamation, betrayal.
Our lethargy.

Enslavement, torture, murder.
Our absence.

Infinite echo of lamentations,
ravaged by pain.

Mountain Scenery

The branches of the firs, with snow upon them,
adopt the position of ballerinas
about to start their dance,
snow nests, snow caps, innumerable.
Blinding expanse of snow, the sunlit slope:
our present life.
The seats of the chair lift
return at regular intervals.
On a sledge
the men of the mountain patrol
are taking a casualty down to the valley.
A strange word: mishap.

In the Jewish Cemetery in Worms

An afternoon spend among names –
Rabbi Baruch, Maharam Mair of Rothenburg,
Maharil Jacob Molin.
An afternoon spent with a few movements
of light on very ancient stones.

Tomb of the Hunt and Fishing at Tarquinia

The man who,
pushing his boat from the bank,
leans overboard
to sink his line in the water –

The man who,
kneeling on a rock,
is about to
aim at the passing birds –

You meet them again
in the Tomb of the Hunt and Fishing
on tufa
on a pale-green base.

The men are frozen
in their attempt
to capture the invisible.

Silent the plateau
as you step out
and the sea across thistles
reaches out for your eyes.

A Piece of Driftwood

The waves
fling
a piece of driftwood
against the rocky coast,
ceaselessly.

It might
be a man.

What I Know

My place of work,
the house, the street, the trees,
the bus stop,
the immediate neighbourhood,
a bare square mile,
the faces of yesterday,
of last week –

that and a little more
is what I know.
What I think I know.

For I can no longer
be certain
that I know it.

How else
can I explain
why I want to see again and again
what I have seen so often.

Eagerly,
with growing curiosity.

Columbus

The other day
I encountered Columbus
in a backstreet of Genoa,
not far from his small house.

He had just
returned from his third voyage.

As for the existence
of a new continent,
he had never really
believed it, he said.

The ancients,
after all, had known nothing about it.

Instead he had sometimes
had the impression
of approaching paradise.

Observation of currents
had suggested the idea to him.

But Castile was more beautiful,
he thought.

If he had in fact
found a new coastline
he wouldn't understand it till later.

At least there's a chance,
he added.

The Earth on a Photograph

Here is the Earth
for the first time,
here a hurricane,
here a cloudbank,
easy to make out,
presumably following
the line of the Andes.

Here is the Earth which
holds and hides life,
a disease of matter,
Suevo called it.

Here is the dusk of nightfall
and here is brightness

from borrowed light,
from far away,
light multitudinous.

Transformations

Even on a day
that is mild
and slips from your hands like a bird
you can no longer be indifferent.

We will communicate
with calls, nutritious like fruit,
and with lights
held out into the night.

Chill of our time –
who could bear it
without observing the transformations
taking place everywhere.

On the Wall of the House

A piece of wall
found by the sun.

A piece of wall
I lean against.

Years of past life
faithfully return
with this sun,
still without pupil.

A piece of wall
in which the afternoon
loses itself without much ado.

But why don't we Scream?

How are we to make sure
we are here?
Leave the house and return?
Draw maps, town plans, views?
Say something? Do say something,
why don't you say something?

The brief history of a body.
Today we are still here,
each visiting his heart like a gallery.
But why don't we scream?
Beginning and end
and the difference between them
which I still don't understand.
And every movement
for the first and last time.

Deserted Village

The skeleton
of a deserted village,
not marked on any map,
crumbling.

Near-by
a man
with a wooden pole
knocking figs off a tree.

Life
continues.

Morning in the City

I

The morning, full of wrinkles,
follows the night as a memory
of a dream
in which someone died.

The streets,
twisted like life,
are alone with themselves.

Later, a start of
half-hearted duels of chrome.

Hopelessness
has its first entrances.

In the sky clouds
in ribbons, white,
hair.

II

Late morning
bleached bones.
On endless pavements
– endless like years –
faces
indifferent, silent,
until one notices the blue rotating light
and the siren of the riot police van.

Rainy Day on the Beach

Think of a country
to live in,
for the seasons
succeed one another most irregularly
as though the earth
had become impatient.

Morning

It approaches
and the air
is full of shouting.

To the edge of the sea
the air
is full of shouting.

Right to the cities
beyond the sea
the air
is full of shouting
which turns to light,
listen –

On Reading Leonardo's Philosophical Diaries

I read
that the bell
retains in itself
the noise of the ring.

That the eye
retains in itself
the images of a luminous body.

That projections are possible
beyond all things.

That proof is worthless
without counterproof.

That the sun
has never
seen any kind of shadow.

That souls
originate from the sun.

That the moon is dense and heavy,
dense and heavy.

That the effect participates
in the cause.

That the air is full of
many straight lines.

That moments are
the terminal points of time.

Michelangelo

Mostly he had difficulties
getting his marble.
Often the blocks did not
turn out as he wished.

Time and again
the dried-up Arno:
the barges unable
to reach Florence.

All those quarrels
with his assistants
who were trying to cheat him.

Of art
he spoke seldom.

He called himself
a foolish
old man.

He thanked his relations
for sending wine and cheese.
Can't think of anything else,
he sometimes concluded
his short letters.

He hoped
that death would
treat him no worse
than other old men.

When he died in Rome
the city would not
hand over his body.

His nephew
had it secretly brought to Florence,
packed as a bale of merchandise
and addressed to Vasari.

Domenico di Bartolo

There you can see him
crossing Siena's Campo.

This week he will
complete his cycle of frescoes,
representing the history
and everyday work of the Hospital,
the enlargement of the building,
the admission of the sick,
the care, education
and marriage of the foundlings.

The woman's face
remains to be painted,
disturbed while drying
her washing in front of the fire.

He'll make her
scowl.

The cycle does not deserve mention,
noted Jacob Burckhardt.

Misfortune

'Free doth misfortune stalk about the earth.'
Schiller: *Wallenstein*

Even darkness
cannot escape it.

Nothing any longer resembles
what hope thought up.

Peace is too far away
to be complacent.

Gaiety avoids the city.

There is a little sunlight
on the avenue,
but soon it dies.

Men busy themselves
with a life
that has not reached them.

Snow

I

Snow,
allusion
to the future.

Future,
vulnerable word.

II

Snow.

Hope has
large eyes.

Aeschylus saw
that they were blind.

Pretexts

We've piled up pretexts
between ourselves and peace.
Else we'd discover it
in the middle of the plain
on which snow is ceaselessly falling:
lonely and ready to approach.

Shadow of Hope

Our hope,
it casts its shadow before it,
there it is.

Can't you see it?
Surely one can see it.

Sometimes it merges
with the other shadows,
the shadows of houses,
of trees.

But a moment later
it can once more be discovered.

It is moving forward.
It is keeping alive.

Wind-blown Sand Everywhere

What we expected
will not come about,
we shall anticipate it.

In any case it becomes
less and less possible
to count on oneself.

That nothing of
what has been shall be lost

that nothing was in vain
even though nothing remains

no rhyme can be found for it.

Everywhere this wind-blown sand,
troublesome to the eyes,
one can scarcely walk.

A Fool

A fool, one says
full of pity, a dreamer,
a poor devil,
if someone
regards gain also as loss,
if he believes
that useless things will survive.
But only the fools
will still achieve anything.

The Child

The child on the edge of the goat track,
as yet without sadness,
as yet without an eye for the fragments,
who thinks of
how yesterday the lark
hung motionless in the air,
will only later understand
that memory
starts anew
with each birth.
Today he sees the poppy
brilliant in the wild oats.

On Returning to our Flat

When, after weeks away,
we return to the flat
the table, the vase,
the telephone sit down with us.
We rediscover their pulse,
the smooth surface of the door,
the roughness of the cooker,
the weight of cupboards and bed.

Morandi

The silence assumes
the outlines of a bowl,
a bottle, a jug,

a space separating
one object
from another,

a shadow
as an echo of light

or a few words:
I have been fortunate
to lead an uneventful life.

The Hangman's House

The hangman's house
in Salzburg,
time immured,
solitary, at the cross-roads,
no one, from fear,
built near it,
no gingerbread baker, no candle maker.
The windows have become blind,
the landscape outside
only seems to be fixed,
it is still in formation,
darkness still lies on it.

Montaigne

Whenever possible
he sneaks up to his library
on the third floor of his tower.

Sixteen paces across,
room for a table
and a chair.
Three windows.

Below him he sees
the garden, stabling, the yard.

He jots down something,
leafs first through one book
then through another,
without plan.

The exercise involved in
reaching the remote
circular chamber
gives him pleasure to the end.

Die Sonne im Dorf

In Schwarz gehüllt waren die Menschen
zwischen den weiß getünchten Häusern
ihres Dorfs in den Bergen.

Der Mann zeigte es uns
mit seinen Wegen, Höfen, Melonen,
seiner ansteckenden Stille.

Seine Worte kamen zum Vorschein
wie Siegel, die man eben
in den Feldern gefunden hatte.

Dan deutete er zur Sonne,
die groß, als sei sie dort befestigt,
zwischen den Dächern stand:

Sie sei die Mitte des Orts,
sie halte alles am Leben,
wir sollten sie nicht übersehen.

The Sun in the Village

Veiled in black were the people
among the whitewashed houses
of their village in the hills.

The man showed it to us
with its paths, farmyards, melons,
its contagious silence.

His words were a sudden presence
like ancient seals only just
turned up among the fields.

Then he pointed to the sun
which, as if fastened there,
stood large between the roofs:

It was, he said, the centre of the village,
it kept everything alive,
we should not overlook it.

Reflection of Flames

One day at noon
– when beings are aware of each other –
the man offered
grapes and pomegranates
to the passing strangers,
invited them into his house,
showed them donkey and wine barrel,
the reticent nut-tree,
then, just across there,
oil derricks and industries
down to the sea.
Later the evening
took hold of the land,
the reflection of flames
in the sky
had many hands.

And So On

How?
Under what conditions?
Words
which speak,
halt,
are silent,
are forgetful,
sham death.

Difficult Crossing

Not only on ships
consisting of
material of greater specific weight
than water.

With the risk
– so much has sunk to the bottom –
of capsizing or running aground.

Comparing
what is and what might be,
what may well become shore.

Don Juan

There will be no punishment
by Heaven.

Only ageing.

Desire
will hammer no more.

The backdrop of years
will be more ghostly,

the flesh will grow cold
and evaporate.

Gislebertus of Autun: Eve

As she takes the apple
and listens

she understands
two bodies as
two waves in harmony,

she knows
that there will never be enough lips
to speak of the transformations,

she suspects
that humans will time and again
exchange
life for death,

she seeks
answers to questions
which no one yet has asked

as she takes the apple
and listens.

From a cycle *Love Poems*

In you
mystery found
its home,
its refuge.

Where else
could it
have turned?

A long time
it strayed about, disguised
among masks.

You did not
refuse it your favour.

You are the house
which I inhabit.

You are the city
in which I'm staying.

You are the country
through which I'm travelling.

A house, a city, a country.

Have a share
in love on earth.

Together see the morning
climbing the roof-tops.

Hear the day
whose calling is stifled by the heat.

Turn to each other
when darkness sucks the hours
till it draws blood.
Bid good-night to each other
in life's core.

————

I want to drive to the sea with you
and hear your voice
which, as an echo,
will linger on the shore for a long time.

You'll be collecting shells
and do your hair
in which the wind ends.

I want to see your exuberance dancing
on the waves
and watch
as you light the evening
with your eyes.

Trap

At first it is just
a line on the horizon.

Now comes another,
it's nearer already.

Soon one perceives
lines everywhere.

They rapidly
draw together.

Too late one discovers
that there is no escape.

Walter Helmut Fritz

born 1929 in Karlsruhe, Germany, lives there and teaches at the university.

Achtsam sein (poems) 1956
Bild und Zeichen (poems) 1958
Veränderte Jahre (poems) 1963
Umwege (prose) 1964
Zwischenbemerkungen (prose) 1964
Abweichung (novel) 1965
Die Zuverlässigkeit der Unruhe (poems) 1966
Bemerkungen zu einer Gegend (prose) 1969
Die Verwechslung (novel) 1970
Aus der Nähe (poems) 1972
Die Beschaffenheit solcher Tage (novel) 1972
Bevor uns Hören und Sehen vergeht (novel) 1975
Schwierige Überfahrt (poems) 1976
Sehnsucht (poems) 1978
Gesammelte Gedichte (poems) 1979

Also radio plays, essays, and translations from the French (Bosquet, Follain, Jaccottet, Ménard, Vigée)

The poems in this volume are from *Veränderte Jahre* (Deutsche Verlagsanstalt, Stuttgart), *Die Zuverlässigkeit der Unruhe, Aus der Nähe* and *Schwierige Überfahrt* (the last three Hoffmann und Campe, Hamburg).

Ewald Osers

born 1917 in Prague, has lived in England since 1938. A volume of his own poems, *Wish You Were Here*, was published in 1976. He has broadcast and lectured on problems of literary translation. In 1971 he received the Schlegel-Tieck Prize for translation from the German, and in 1977 the International C.B. Nathhorst Translation Prize.

Modern Czech Poetry (with J. K. Montgomery)
    Allen & Unwin, London 1945

Three Czech Poets (V. Nezval, A. Bartušek, J. Hanzlík)
    Penguin Books, London 1970

Selected Poems by Ondra Lysohorsky
    Cape Editions, London 1971;
    Grossman Publishers Inc., New York 1971

Underseas Possessions: Selected Poems by Hans-Jürgen Heise
    Oleander Press, New York and Cambridge, England 1972

With the Volume Turned Down & Other Poems by Reiner Kunze
    London Magazine Editions, London 1973

The Aztec Calendar & Other Poems by Antonín Bartušek
    Anvil Press, London 1975;
    Iowa Translation Series, Iowa 1975

Contemporary German Poetry
    Oleander Press, New York and Cambridge, England 1976

Strawberries in December & Other Poems by Hans Dieter Schäfer
    Carcanet Press, Cheadle 1976

Selected Poems by Rose Ausländer
    London Magazine Editions, London 1977

Wounded No Doubt: Selected Poems by Rudolf Langer
    Menard Press, London 1979

The Plague Column by Jaroslav Seifert
    Terra Nova Editions, London & Boston 1979

1001 Hayrens by Nahapet Kuchak (Medieval Armenian love lyrics)
    Sovetakan Grogh, Erevan 1979

Umbrella from Piccadilly by Jaroslav Seifert
    Terra Nova Editions (in preparation)

Not Marked on the Map by Hanns Cibulka
    Terra Nova Editions (in preparation)

Selected Poems by Miroslav Válek
    Tatran, Bratislava (in preparation)